The Way Of The Kingdom

Understanding Faith, The Church, And The Christian Life

Written By:
Justin & Elly Heckel
Ann Lenaers

Contents

The Jail Cell

The Lord is not slow in keeping his promise,
as some understand slowness.
Instead he is patient with you,
not wanting anyone to perish,
but everyone to come to repentance.
2 Peter 3:9

There is a burning question commonly asked by believers and unbelievers alike - why would a good God send people to hell? The truth is we serve a God who is fair, just, and righteous. His every act aims to redeem what has gone wrong and make us whole again. His heart's desire isn't for anyone to go to hell - it's simply for our hearts to join with His to right the wrongs and walk with Him in perfect unity. The problem is that we are helpless to do this by ourselves.

Another question you may have asked: Why can't I just do a bunch of good things and be a good person to get into heaven? Well, let's open these questions up...

Because the first man and woman committed what we call original sin, *all* humans are born into sin. Sin occurs when you act contrary to your conscience while pursuing what you understand to be the Lord's will. Some say it is missing the mark or making bad choices. In general, Romans 13:10 suggests sin is when we act outside of love and cause harm, so it is only fair that we are accountable for our sins. There are consequences, a price to be paid.

It's like we are born into a jail cell. People try to follow all sorts of religious routes, like trying to pray enough or going to church enough. If they believe in another religion, they think they need to complete certain tasks. But the officer guarding your cell is standing there with the registry, unmoved if they don't get the right answer.

If you say, "Let me out," he's going to ask why. If you say Muhammed, your priest, or your pastor told you such and such, the officer will look and say, "I'm sorry, I have no record of them having authority to get you out." If your reasoning is, "I have done so many good things," he will reply with, "I'm sorry. You have not done enough good things to get out."

The only answer that will suffice is, "Jesus paid for me to get out."

He is the only one with authority and the only one who has paid the price. This is the Good News (the Gospel). When nobody else was able to do anything to get me out of this prison - hell - Jesus was willing to give it all for us to be free.

A lot of people will laugh and say, "Oh yeah, that imaginary prison cell." But it's *real*. It's just not physical. We know it's real and that it isn't only a future destination. God is powerful, wise, free, and prosperous, and you would expect that His children would look like that as well. That was His original design for us, but sin pulls us away from it. This *spiritual* jail cell looks like fears, doubt, guilt, shame, and rejection. Have you experienced these things?

We all have. When we do, it causes us to live in a way that is less than what God has intended for us. He wants us to walk in unity with Him, to have peace, and to have joy as part of His family. His desire is that we would look like Him on this earth, so He showed us the Way to get there through Jesus.

The bottom line is, no matter what other options we might like to try, there is only one way to come back into right relationship with God and enter His house. As the owner of the house, God is allowed to choose the correct way to enter. I know if a friend knocks on my door at a reasonable time, I will lovingly greet them and let them in. If they try to break in through the kitchen window at 3am, they will be met with police, handcuffs, and a ride to jail.

God appointed us to enter through a specific door and named it Jesus.

The Core Gospel

*I am the door; if anyone enters through Me,
he will be saved, and will go in and out
and find pasture.
The thief comes only to steal and kill and destroy;
I came that they may have life,
and have it abundantly.*
John 10:9-10 (NASB 1995)

In the beginning, we all walked and talked face-to-face with God, but sin created a gap between us. Ever since then, every culture and people group wanted to believe that they knew who God was, how life worked, how to navigate the ups and downs, and that one day when life is done, we get to go somewhere far from all the troubles to live with God forever.

But everyone was making horrible guesses. Our limited minds couldn't understand the limitless perfection of the living God. So at the appointed time, God came as a man named Jesus to take away all of our guessing. He was the very representation of the invisible God. We no longer need to guess what He thinks, how He would respond to things, or how He would speak to us, because He showed it to us in the life of Jesus.

He lived just like us, facing every temptation and challenge we do, but He did it *perfectly*. He was accompanied by miracles, signs, and wonders as He traveled around teaching. Then He went to the cross to die in our place and pay the penalty for our sin, trading His life for ours. He died so that all the old stuff (sin, fear, guilt, shame) could be buried and so that whoever believes in Him would rise with Him to new life.

Many people want Jesus as their Savior, but they do not want Him as their Lord. We all want a superhero who will save us from eternal punishment, but not many like to hand authority over their life to someone else. If we make Him our Lord, giving Him the authority to tell us how to live this new life, the Bible says that He saves us on Judgment Day. So to receive Him as our Lord and Savior is an exchange. He gave His life for us, so we no longer live our own lives but let Him live through us. Who better to be in charge of our lives than one who loves perfectly?!

After Jesus rose from the dead, He was seen by many over the course of 40 days. Before ascending to the Father, He told His disciples that when He left, the Father would send us the Holy Spirit. He told them that the Holy Spirit was exactly like Him. This means that when we speak with the Holy Spirit, we can speak to Him just like the disciples talked with Jesus.

Today when we declare Jesus as Lord over our lives and commit to follow him, we can receive the Holy Spirit both in us and upon us. He is in us for our sake, giving us peace, joy, boldness, etc. He is upon us for the sake of others, so people will ask for prayer, healing, etc. The Spirit loves to glorify Jesus, and He does a better job at it than any minister on earth.

The Holy Spirit is the Spirit of the Father and the Spirit of Jesus Christ. He has some big jobs to do with us. He teaches us regarding all things, leads us into all truth, and reminds us of what Jesus has said. He also speaks through us when we don't know what to say and prays for us when we don't know what to pray. He empowers us to glorify Jesus, and He comforts us in our time of need.

So again, the Good News is that Jesus gave His life for us. But He didn't just save us to go to heaven after waiting out the hard parts of life. He refused to leave us alone and sent His very Spirit to come live inside us while we are still here on earth.

There's a saying that each of us has a God-sized hole in our hearts. As many have experienced, you will come to find this space is just waiting for our *yes* to the Holy Spirit, and it aches like something is missing in our lives until it is filled. When we don't understand the source of this problem, we often try to fill the void or dull the ache by chasing all the world has to offer, but it is never enough.

When you receive the Spirit and become a home for it, the ache stops and is replaced with the only thing that can make us whole, complete, and truly satisfied. Everything else on this earth tries to throw things at you to make it all better. The Holy Spirit is the only thing in existence that heals from the inside out.

What is sin and how does it work?

Sin works like this. One day my oldest son hit his younger brother for the first time. It was the first time he was really in trouble. Just minutes before, we had been playing together, and he was loving spending time with his dad. But now, I yelled his name across the room. A look of terror came over his face. He ran and hid behind the couch and began to cry. I called his name and gently said, "Come here, bud," but he tried to stay hidden. Immediately, it hit me...Adam.

The voice of Dad, who had been playing with you and making you food had now become a source of fear. You ran and hid. Dad still showed up, still pursued, but your sin made you run and hide. I called out, not because I didn't know where you were physically, but I wanted you to tell me where you were mentally so that we could address it together.

In many ways, the human condition is to still react just like Adam and Eve. But did God leave us or create separation because of our sin? No! We did that! If Satan was already here, then we were placed into a situation that already had potential for confusion.

It's as though I took my kids to a carnival to have fun as a family. Let's say while we were there, my oldest son hit one of my other sons. Imagine I said, "That's it! I'm leaving you here alone in this confusion where anything else can happen to you." I would probably get my kids taken away from me. I would be a horrible parent for that, but many of us have been taught to assign that attribute to God.

Instead, what if I swat my son, spank him, or discipline him however it seems fit? I know that in his frustration and anger he would try to run and get away from the family. He would try to create distance, but I would need to hold his hand so that he couldn't. I know my son. He would turn his back to my back so that in his mind he would create a gap between us. It's like Paul says in Colossians 1:21, that we became enemies of God in our minds because of our evil behavior.

So we're at a carnival. Being a good dad, I'm not going to let one person ruin the day for everyone. So I start moving the family along to the next attraction or ride. The whole time, I'm holding my son's hand so he doesn't run off. In his mind, we're still back in that moment five or ten minutes ago when the incident occurred - but I'm not. I just want the family to have a good time together and for him to be his fun self again.

This is so much like what sin does to us and how the Father feels toward us in our sin. Our sin is what destroyed us. It made us create a gap in our minds between us and Him. Our sin is what makes us think our Father doesn't love us, so we get even angrier. But He isn't stuck on when you did this or that! His discipline comes upon us so that we grow *because*

He loves us, but all He is actually wanting is for us to stay with the family and enjoy His goodness! We repent (meaning to turn away from that sin toward God) and are forgiven, and He remembers it no more. We are the ones who have a hard time letting go.

What happened on the cross?

So much of our traditions line up with Jesus taking our punishment as though God needed a whipping boy or He couldn't possibly forgive us. If that were the case, it wouldn't be forgiveness. It would be revenge. The wages of sin is death - meaning if you work for sin, you get paid with death. Jesus wasn't paying the price to God, but paying the price to sin. How does this make sense? Let's break it down.

Being perfect and sinless, Jesus had absolutely zero need to die on the cross for us. Yet, apparently there was a deep need for Him to die exactly the way He did, because He asked the Father in the Garden of Gethsemane if there was another way. Apparently there wasn't. So why did it so badly need to happen this way? Because *we* were the ones who needed Him to die like that. Out of His great love for us, He considered it pure joy to please the Father and bring us back into full relationship with the Trinity (the Father, Son, and Holy Spirit).

Why did we need this? Because otherwise, we never would have believed He forgave us! We were the adulterers, murderers, thieves, etc! We were the ones who liked to flaunt ourselves as know-it-alls when we knew nothing. Meanwhile, He came in meekness and humility! We were the ones who deserved to be mocked, spit on, beaten, wear a crown of thorns, carry our cross, and be nailed up on it bare to die.

When we sinned, we ran, hid, and tried to cover ourselves up. But when Jesus took on all the sin of the whole world that ever existed or ever would exist, He made sure that He was hung up bare in front of everyone where He could not get away from people seeing it. He took on all our guilt and all our shame.

This is why it says He despised the shame of the cross. He was feeling how we had felt all this time. He hated that we felt like running, hiding, and covering up. He hated that we felt distant. If Jesus hadn't taken our place like that, we never would have believed we were forgiven. It wasn't just about getting the Father to forgive us but about getting us to believe we were forgiven.

Imagine you murdered a guy's son. Then imagine this dad came and forgave you. Would you truly believe it? Probably not. Then imagine he told you he was giving you a car and some money. You would most likely feel like it was a set up for a bigger plan against you, right? Then if he came and took you out to eat, you would be certain that at some point he would be taking you out into a field to leave you for dead. *BUT* if someone else wanted revenge on you and this dad took a bullet and died to save your life, you would probably start to believe he really forgave you.

See, it's not just that Jesus took our punishment for us. It's that He let us give Him the punishment that was meant for us. We needed it in order that we might believe we had been forgiven. In fact, Paul tells us that when Jesus was on the cross, the Father was inside of Him reconciling the world to Himself.

How can I know that I am saved?

Many people ask this question, and it can be difficult if we base it on anything other than God, His works, and His word. It can't be based on our own works or feelings. However, the presence of God in our lives will produce a new nature in us that shows we are saved. That transformation is part of the evidence that shows your faith is sincere.

The quick answer is found in Romans 10:9 which says, *"If you declare with your mouth, "Jesus is Lord," and believe in your heart that God raised him from the dead, you will be saved."* As was said about getting out of the jail cell, the only sufficient answer is that Jesus paid for me to get out, and He is the one I am following.

The other piece of the answer is found in John 6:44, *"No one can come to me unless the Father who sent me draws them, and I will raise them up at the last day."* We can't even desire to come to Jesus unless the Father first draws us. It may simply start with us having that desire, or it could be a desire that rises up from somebody talking about Jesus. Either way, we can't even have that desire unless He first draws us.

John 15:16 says, *"You did not choose me, but I chose you and appointed you so that you might go and bear fruit - fruit that will last - and so that whatever you ask in my name the Father will give you."* So Jesus chose us first, and it was so that we would bear good fruit. That means the question is not did Jesus choose me and provide salvation for me, but have I actually responded to Him and chosen to walk in His ways?

What Is Kingdom Citizenship?

*For the kingdom of God
is not a matter of eating and drinking,
but of righteousness, peace and joy
in the Holy Spirit.*
Romans 14:17

C.S. Lewis said, "The Son of God became a man to enable men to become sons of God." When we are born naturally, our bodies are alive, but our spirits are dead because of sin. When we are born again, we are given a new, alive spirit. But many like to call themselves believers without knowing what it means to be a believer.

If a friend of your child comes over and is respectful of the rules of your house, you would probably let them be around a lot and sometimes make statements such as, "They're like my own child." However, if your child's friend comes over and doesn't respect the rules of your house, you will probably limit their access and not claim they are like a second child to you. Many people like to say they are friends of Jesus, but Jesus told his disciples He called them friends because they did what He commanded them. Many people like to say they are children of God, but Jesus said the ones who are His mother, sisters, and brothers are the ones who do the will of His Father.

As American Citizens, we have a certain group identity. Even when you are in other countries, people can often easily point you out and declare that you're an American. As a citizen, we know what laws must be obeyed, but we also know what rights we have and feel free to express them. We also know that we may forfeit certain rights when we break certain laws.

Paul tells us in Romans 14:17 that **the Kingdom of Heaven is righteousness, peace, and joy in the Holy Spirit**. As Kingdom Citizens, that is what we get to walk in. I would also add things like boldness, forgiveness, humility, authority, freedom, and power. These things are at the core of our new identity.

As a Kingdom Citizen, there are two main Commandments that take care of everything we need to follow:

Love God and love your neighbor as yourself.

Love is the only verb in these two commands that everything hangs from, so the whole Bible is defining what that word really means from heaven's perspective. We quickly realize as we learn divine nature that the world does not define love the same way God does, so we need to adapt into the culture of His Kingdom.

When those commands are broken, we start seeing our inheritance as a Kingdom Citizen as being hard to hold onto. Our selfish ambitions, pride, ego, unforgiveness, and sense of revenge make it so we start losing our peace, joy and righteousness (alignment with the Lord).

The great part is that God has no desire to punish us for these things. He wants to reconcile and restore us, because at one time He died for every sin that ever happened or would happen. He disciplines us because He does everything with a heart of love to mature us to look like Him. So when we let go of the things that are not of the Kingdom, ask forgiveness, and return to the identity and commands of the Kingdom, we quickly watch the benefits of our citizenship be restored. It's not that He takes away those rights - it's that we feel unworthy to grasp them, so we live in a lesser state, operating outside of our identity.

You need to know that this citizenship is a matter of being a New Creation. God's plan is not a multiple step plan of self-improvement. His plan is to die with Christ and be raised new. As a new creation we are not to be sin-focused as much as we are God-focused. We have a new nature.

Some people will say, "How come I struggle with sin?" That's great! The fact that you are struggling with it is a sign that you have a new nature. We don't struggle against what is in our nature, but what is against our nature.

You used to love your sin and defend it. Now you struggle with it, hate it, and want it out of your life. Conversely, now you love serving people and spending time with the Lord. It bothers you when you don't make time for that, because it is in your nature and you want to do it. A fish doesn't struggle with being in water because it's their nature, but it struggles with being out of water.

Righteousness - our new nature - can be difficult to live in at first, because we have been so conditioned to look at sin instead of at God. But this new nature is very freeing. It's like if you never wore a suit before, and you put one on for a day. It can feel like this isn't who you really are or that it's only for a special day. But for someone whose life involves wearing a suit every day, they simply believe that looking upscale is normal. I invite you to keep wearing your identity of righteousness constantly. In Christ, we are the righteousness of God.

**Welcome to the Kingdom.
Welcome to your new nature.**

Why Do We Pray?

Rejoice always, pray continually,
give thanks in all circumstances;
for this is God's will for you in Christ Jesus.
1 Thessalonians 5:16-18

We tend to make the concept of prayer really hard, but it's actually very simple. It is communication with the Divine. One of the most fundamental actions that shows your faith is sincere is to act on your belief that He will hear you and will answer as the Bible says.

We often think of venting our list of needs and wants over and over, but Jesus said that is a sign of someone who doesn't truly know the Father. Many people treat Him like a God-sized vending machine, where you insert your dollar sized prayer, press a button, retrieve your blessing, and walk away. But He is alive and real, with a heart just like you. If you don't like when someone claims they are your friend but only calls you when they need something, then why would we treat God that way?

Remember, we have been given the Holy Spirit to live inside of us. He is exactly like Jesus. So we can ask Him things exactly like we would ask Jesus. But He is also the Spirit of the Father and the Son, so we can know that when we are praying in the power of the Holy Spirit, that He is helping us be one with Jesus and the Father and to speak like They speak.

We're going to mention "prayer time" here. But just like new love, even though there should be some time to focus, we should come to a place where we're constantly speaking with the Lord throughout the entire day. A lot of our prayer time should simply be consciously dwelling with the Lord, staring at Him, thanking Him, and giving Him glory.

Think about how when someone finds new love, they sicken everyone around them with their constant declarations of affection toward each other. It's the same thing with someone who is captivated by the Lord. They can't shut up about Him or His goodness - not out of obligation, but out of the natural expressions of gratitude and adoration. Even when they get into prayer, they constantly thank Him and tell Him He is wonderful.

Prayer is really for *us*. All of our practices are. God needs nothing from us. If I went to a rich and powerful man to get financial help and advice, it would be wise of me to let him do most of the talking. It is always wise to listen as much as we speak, if not more.

When I spend time with the Lord, I should come out with fruit that looks like love, joy, peace, patience, kindness, goodness, faithfulness, gentleness, and self-control. It's ok to be completely honest and vulnerable with God in prayer, even if you are angry or frustrated. He already sees it all anyway, so there's nothing you can truly hide from Him. Meet Him in your secret place and know that it is a safe place to freely be yourself. But if I come *out* of my prayer time with the Lord and I have anger, fear, or timidity, it is a clear sign I probably spent most of the time simply venting to the Lord.

We become like whoever we love the most and spend the most time with. My goal with every prayer time is to come out differently than when I went in. We want to come out looking more like our Father who is the image of perfect love that casts out all fear. It is truly marvelous to think the God of the universe in all His power and wisdom and glory not only desires but *has* a deeply personal, intimate relationship with you. Cherish that relationship, that gift, and speak with Him.

If you're wondering where to start, the disciples had the same question for Jesus. He answered in Matthew 6:9-13 with what is commonly called the Lord's Prayer. You may have heard it before:

Our Father in heaven, hallowed be Your name. Your Kingdom come, your will be done, on earth as it is in heaven. Give us this day our daily bread, and forgive us our trespasses, as we forgive those who trespass against us. Lead us not into temptation, but deliver us from evil. For Yours is the kingdom, and the power, and the glory forever and ever. Amen

Given what we've said here about prayer, consider that this was never intended to be a copy/paste regurgitation. It is certainly lovely to recite it as written when you cherish the message, but even deeper than that, it was meant to point us to the heart of the Father. It reflects reverence, gratitude, provision, surrender to God's will, forgiveness, and the goodness of heaven being made manifest on this earth through us. We were never meant to wait for death to experience heaven. We were meant to bring heaven here. Lock in on connecting with God's heart in your prayer and mountains will move.

Why Do We Worship?

Praise the Lord, my soul;
all my inmost being, praise his holy name.
Praise the Lord, my soul, and forget not all his benefits -
who forgives all your sins and heals all your diseases,
who redeems your life from the pit
and crowns you with love and compassion,
who satisfies your desires with good things
so that your youth is renewed like the eagle's.
Psalm 103:1-5

All of creation was made to worship, so we are creatures of worship. We all worship something - you can't hide what you worship because you become like what you worship. If you worship money, people will know. If you worship lust, people will know.

Many people think God simply commands us to worship only Him because He is the only one worthy of it, as if He has an ego. But God is not self-seeking. If you won the lottery, nobody would need to tell you to be excited. You would just be filled with joy that would cause you to yell, dance, jump, and sing! Likewise, nobody in Heaven will need to be told to worship. Even in the scriptures, whenever the glory of Jesus was revealed, people fell down in worship as a natural response. The elders in Revelation 4:10-11 cast the crowns that God gave to them at His feet to worship. They weren't forced. When we see the holiness of God and His goodness toward us that we don't deserve to be part of, it causes us to worship.

On a deeper level, He also knows intimately well how He made us, and that we become like what we worship. So He tells us to have no other gods and to worship Him only because we were made to be like Him. Just like prayer, worship is really for our sake. He doesn't need anything from anybody, including our worship. When we, who were made to be loved, encounter the One Who is perfect love without needing us to earn it, we watch the striving and pain that comes from trying to earn it fade and simply get caught up in the pure joy, humility, and reverence of being in His presence.

Musical worship is a powerful tool, but we have greatly limited the definition and expression of worship because of it. Worship should be a part of everything we do. What I complain about, the Lord cannot bless, but He can bless what I worship Him for. So whether I am taking care of my kids, spending time with my spouse, paying my bills, or doing my dishes, I want to be worshiping Him in everything.

An easy breakdown of what praise and worship means: Praise is declaring the goodness of God, and worship is honoring that goodness. "I know You are wise, powerful, loving, etc., so I will act in accordance with that." There are also times we worship through pain. This is very precious to God, because we won't have that opportunity in heaven. But the majority of our worship should simply be a response of thankfulness for who God is and all the good things He does.

This also means that when you share your testimony or give glory to God in ministry, these are also forms of worship that point to our thankfulness for Him. Romans 1:25 references people who exchanged the truth of God for a lie as they worshipped the creation over the Creator. We must always be certain that we are giving credit where it is properly due. Rocks make nothing – God made the rocks.

Additionally, when we gather in corporate worship, we see an atmosphere shift. Time and again, the Spirit of the Lord is evident among us. We feel vulnerable to cry or release our burdens. We are emboldened to share a scripture, give a prophetic word, or pray over each other. The sense of unity and peace greatly heightens because our own desires are collectively put aside to let the desires of the Lord take first place. The result of corporate worship should be greater unity and a group of people that all look like the One they are worshiping. If you find yourself passionate about worship, a great next step would be to read our book "Worship Everywhere."

Why Do We Go To Church?

And let us consider how we may
spur one another on toward love and good deeds,
not giving up meeting together,
as some are in the habit of doing,
but encouraging one another –
and all the more as you see the Day approaching.
Hebrews 10:24-25

Modern culture has greatly confused the idea of the Church, and many of the responses to it have been just as damaging. I want to start by saying what the Church is not - it is not a building.

God does not care where you gather. The Church is really the people the Holy Spirit dwells in - the Body of believers. Nobody can be the Church by themselves, it is a collective. There isn't one gathering place that is the full expression of the Church. In the Bible, there is little mention of how people would gather at this place or that place. When the Church is addressed, it's to the Church of that city.

According to the scripture's description of the Church and what I believe easily rings true in our spirits when heard, the Church gathered daily everywhere - in homes, synagogues (church buildings), and in the market place. The Church saw itself as one in the Lord. So if you hurt, I hurt. If you rejoice, I rejoice. If you have a need, I want to meet it. They constantly encouraged one another and pushed each other in the ways of Jesus.

Two great breakdowns of what the early Church looked like when it was doing well are:

- Acts 2:42-47 - *They devoted themselves to the apostles' teaching and to fellowship, to the breaking of bread and to prayer. Everyone was filled with awe at the many wonders and signs performed by the apostles. All the believers were together and had everything in common. They sold property and possessions to give to anyone who had need. Every day they continued to meet together in the temple courts. They broke bread in their homes and ate together with glad and sincere hearts, praising God and enjoying the favor of all the people. And the Lord added to their number daily those who were being saved.*

- Acts 4:32-35 - *All the believers were one in heart and mind. No one claimed that any of their possessions was their own, but they shared everything they had. With great power the apostles continued to testify to the resurrection of the Lord Jesus. And God's grace was so powerfully at work in them all that there were no needy persons among them. For from time to time those who owned land or houses sold them, brought the money from the sales and put it at the apostles' feet, and it was distributed to anyone who had need.*

We see here that they devoted themselves to the teachings of the leaders. They ate together and took communion. They prayed together and provided their resources freely to take care of each other's needs. They saw miracles done among them. It caused them to praise God and enjoy the favor of those among them.

The unity that happens among a Church truly seeking the Lord causes even outsiders to wonder. It's easy for us to see in our time as we watch people separate over simple differences. When people see a group who knows they don't always agree on everything but refuses to stop loving each other, it causes them to take notice.

There are two sides to the Church that we like to point out. There is the governmental side of the Church that trains and equips the saints to do the work of

Christ in the Church. You can gain a lot of head knowledge and impartation here. Then there is the family side of the Church. This is where we are simply doing life together, truly knowing each other, and holding each other accountable. Training helps us know what to do, but it's when I see you going through tough times that I can see if you let your peace and joy be stolen. It takes both sides for us to truly be the Church.

Community has benefits and responsibilities. Too often in the modern Church we see people enjoying the benefits but ignoring the responsibilities. Part of this is our devotion to holy love among the brethren. We must want to keep the indulgence of sin out from among us. There may be stumbling, and there is grace for earnest walking with Christ. It is when people love their sin that we cannot allow it to stay among us, because a little bit starts working its way through the whole group. What one generation tolerates, the next generation celebrates.

But it is about more than sin. It is the continual desire to outdo one another in love, to know that we have an unpayable debt to Jesus to love His Church like He does. He uses terms of affection for the Church, such as His Bride or Beloved. We must take care of it with Him in mind, remembering that we are one in Christ.

What Is God's Design For Family?

God lives eternally as the Trinity, one God in three persons. People wonder how this can be possible. In many ways it is mysterious to us, and the closest thing that can come to it is the family unit. This is why He gave us the family as the first institution to represent God to us. They dwell as separate people, and yet they are one.

When people refer to me, they almost always understand that they are also referring to my spouse. Additionally, when we say someone is a certain way, we naturally expect their children are going to be similar.

How do we treat our spouse?

Let's first look at marriage. Marriage is intended to be an image of Christ and the Church. Men are supposed to love their wife as Christ loved the Church, laying His life down for it. In today's culture, we must be cautious about the way we frame this. A man is not to be domineering, but He is to be the spiritual leader of the house. The same way that he is to make sure the house is provided for and protected, he is also to do that spiritually.

He is doing this to create a safe place for the wife to cultivate the inside of the home and make the home prosperous. Just like the Church is called to make disciples, the wife is creating a place conducive for the discipling of the children. The goal is for them to be able to grow physically, mentally, and spiritually, to move out, and to have a home of their own one day.

Just as it is important for the husband to love the wife, it is important for the wife to respect her husband. He is often carrying burdens that he doesn't typically discuss because it isn't his nature. But if the house falls apart, even if it's because of a decision she made, people will look at the husband and wonder why he couldn't take care of his family. So it is important that she consider him in her decisions just as he is to consider her. They are to be two sides making the whole. The Bible says that when they chose each other, they became one.

What about our children?

It is said that 90% of who you'll be as an adult is formed by age seven, so the earlier we start training our children for success in life, the better. If we wait until they're about ready to move out to teach them skills and good habits, the chances of them continuing them are slim. But if we start teaching them at a young age, they are not likely to depart because they see the goodness that comes with it. We've given them proper time to process, apply, and experience these good things under our care and supervision.

In this way, the family unit acts as one. The father makes sure outside forces are optimal for the family. The mother does the same with the inside forces, and the children grow in their ability to contribute.

We must also remember that teaching and training a child is just as much about what they observe us doing as it is what we tell them, if not more. Have you ever watched a child play with dolls and act out their parents' and siblings' behaviors with them? Sometimes that mirror is sweet, and sometimes you feel super called out, because you realize they learned by watching you. When a child sees the fruit of your faith - the strength, love, peace, joy, wisdom, community, and stability it gives you - they will aspire to have that for themselves. They will watch what you do to get it and copy you, absorbing their environment like a sponge.

It's important that we bring our children along in our faith and give them more credit for what they're capable of learning and doing. Jesus said to let the little children come to him! We cannot tell them church is about community, prayer, worship, service, mercy, and so many other awesome benefits but then only plant them in front of cartoons with Bible stories designed for short attention spans in Sunday school and think that is enough. Children are most often hands-on, experiential learners, so we need to actively engage them in healthy Christian culture.

We have seen toddlers pray for someone's healing in their beautiful childlike faith. We see elementary children share the gospel with their friends, write their own worship songs, and give powerful words of wisdom at the most Spirit-led times. We see high schoolers serve, evangelize, lead worship, start ministries, and do foreign missions. Be the shoulders the next generation can stand on and let them come to Him.

Why Does Church Have Traditions?

"This is my body, which is for you;
do this in remembrance of me."
1 Corinthians 11:24

As you will see in any longstanding culture, the Church has some beautiful, meaningful traditions that have been passed down through generations. The problems start when we treat them like an obligation, a required checkmark we must begrudgingly endure to avoid an angry God or social judgment. That is not the plan or purpose for these experiences.

At the core, these practices are intended to be heartfelt reminders of important components of our faith. We do them over and over, year after year, so that we never forget what really matters. If you treat these activities as nothing more than a task, you will miss out on the richness of your faith. If you let the Holy Spirit lead you through them in your heart, they will give you even deeper roots in your relationship with the Lord, as well as strengthen your connections in the Body.

What are common Christian traditions you will encounter?

Baby Dedication

Dedicating a baby is when the parents bring their child before God and express their desire for the Lord to cover, bless, and walk with their child for life. The family and community gather and make a commitment to the Lord to see this child as a gift that they will faithfully steward. It is common for a leader in the church to anoint the child's head with oil and pray a blessing over them. Since the child cannot yet make their own decision to follow Christ, the community is committing with the parents to guide the child in the way they should go until they are old enough to make that decision for themselves.

Baptism

This is one of the main sacraments - an outward sign of inward grace, a covenant with God, and a means of regeneration. The Holy Spirit will often signal you when you're ready for this step. Today many people argue over how this should be done, but the teachings of the Apostles clearly state that whether a person is fully submerged in water or being sprinkled, it is still baptism if the belief is in a new life through Jesus Christ. It's about the spiritual, not the physical.

Some symbols tied to it from the Old Testament are:
- the Ark carrying Noah and His family through the destruction of all the evil in the world
- the Red Sea parting for Israel to pass through while devouring the Egyptian army that was coming after them
- the mikvah - a Jewish ritual bath in "living water" meant to purify

Likewise, it's a symbol that you have passed from death to life, and the spiritual enemy that enslaved you your entire life doesn't get to come along. Romans 6 paints a clear image that we have died and risen with Christ, and now it is no longer us who lives, but Christ who lives through us.

Prior to baptizing someone, there are some basic concepts we want to confirm the person being baptized understands:
- We were born into sin and headed to hell.
- Jesus is the only way to the Father and Heaven.
- When Jesus died, He did away with the old creation.
- When we believe Jesus died for us and repent of our own ways, turning from dark to light, we are raised to being a new creation.
- He gives His Holy Spirit to live in us as a down payment of the fullness we will experience in Heaven.
- He is coming back again and will save those who have believed in His name.

The one who is baptizing the person will ask:
- Do you receive and agree with what you've heard of the Gospel here?
- Do you receive Jesus as your Lord and Savior and turn from your own ways?

Then the person being baptized will want to cross their arms on their chest and plug their nose before going under the water, and we will baptize them in the name of the Father, the Son, and the Holy Spirit. Now, not only do you know what to expect when you get baptized, but you also know how simple it is to act on your faith and baptize someone else yourself.

Communion (The Lord's Supper)

Communion is another main sacrament demonstrating that we are nourished from the blood and body of Christ. Jesus asked us to do this in remembrance of him when He ate his last meal with the disciples before He went to the cross. It is His work and His life that gives us life. When we eat the bread and drink the wine (or grape juice) in communion, it is important for us to examine ourselves to see if there is anything unrepentant in us. Scripture says that when we take communion we are declaring the Lord's death until He returns. When we declare that the Lord died, we are also declaring our freedom from sin because that was given through His death. So if we are in unrepentant sin, we are actually declaring that we have been set free from sin but are choosing to do it willingly. Paul mentions that many people actually died in the early Church from taking communion in an unworthy manner.

Celebrating Holidays

There are two main Christian holidays - Christmas and Easter - with differing views about celebrating them. You should practice as you feel led, but do not force things upon each other. These holidays have become widely popular and commercialized over time, so we often see unbelievers celebrate them as well; however, they were originally intended to help us remember the biggest moments of our faith's history - Christ coming to earth (Christmas) and Him conquering sin and death on the cross (Easter). You will find the heart of the gospel and rich value studying the birth and death of Jesus. Let Him be your focal point.

There were also seven major holidays given to Israel in the Old Testament (with Hanukkah as a minor and therefore optional eighth). These were given as remembrances of the Lord's faithfulness to Israel but also as prophetic pictures of what would ultimately be fulfilled in Jesus. Christians do not typically practice them, but there is no place that says Christians can't, shouldn't, or must participate. When practiced, they give a deeper understanding as to what some of the scriptures are speaking about.

Reciting Creeds

There have been over 150 different creeds written throughout Christian history. They help us remember the core unifying tenants of our faith in God. It's helpful because we often get too complex in our thinking, which also often leads to debates. Creeds help bring our focus back to the important parts.

We can become mechanical about reciting creeds if we are not taking them to heart. *However,* if you truly allow yourself to be present with the words and thoughtfully consider what you are saying, they can be a powerful practice that grounds us in the most solid foundations of our faith. Two of the most common creeds are:

- **Apostles' Creed** - I believe in God, the Father almighty, Creator of heaven and earth, and in Jesus Christ, his only Son, our Lord, who was conceived by the Holy Spirit, born of the Virgin Mary, suffered under Pontius Pilate, was crucified, died and was buried; he descended into hell; on the third day he rose again from the dead; he ascended into heaven, and is seated at the right hand of God the Father almighty; from there he will come to judge the living and the dead. I believe in the Holy Spirit, the holy catholic Church, the communion of saints, the forgiveness of sins, the resurrection of the body, and life everlasting. Amen.

- **Nicene Creed** - I believe in one God, the Father almighty, maker of heaven and earth, of all things visible and invisible.

  I believe in one Lord Jesus Christ, the Only Begotten Son of God, born of the Father before all ages. God from God, Light from Light, true God from true God, begotten, not made, consubstantial with the Father; through him all things were made. For us men and for our salvation he came down from heaven, and by the Holy Spirit was incarnate of the Virgin Mary, and became man. For our sake he was crucified under Pontius Pilate, he suffered death and was buried, and rose again on the third day in accordance with the Scriptures. He ascended into heaven and is seated at the right hand of the Father. He will come again in glory to judge the living and the dead and his kingdom will have no end.

  I believe in the Holy Spirit, the Lord, the giver of life, who proceeds from the Father and the Son, who with the Father and the Son is adored and glorified, who has spoken through the prophets. I believe in one, holy, catholic and apostolic Church. I confess one Baptism for the forgiveness of sins and I look forward to the resurrection of the dead and the life of the world to come. Amen.

At His Presence Church, we recite a special consecration prayer we have developed as a reminder and affirmation of our surrender to Christ:

Lord, this is Your mind.
It doesn't get to think whatever it wants.
It only gets to think what You think.
Lord, this is Your heart.
It doesn't get to have affections for whatever it wants.
Teach me to love what You love
and hate what You hate.
Lord, these are Your eyes.
They don't get to look at whatever they want.
Let them see the things You see.
Lord, these are Your ears.
Block them from hearing things
that aren't meant for me.
Let me hear Your voice clearly.
Lord, this is Your mouth.
It doesn't get to say whatever it wants.
It only gets to say what You say.
Lord, these are Your hands.
Let them do Your work.
Lord, my feet are Your feet.
Lead me into divine encounters
to be blessed and be a blessing.
I am not my own. I was bought with a price.
Do with me what You will to bring You glory and honor.

Why Do We Serve?

Neither do people light a lamp and put it under a bowl.
Instead they put it on its stand,
and it gives light to everyone in the house.
In the same way, let your light shine before others,
that they may see your good deeds
and glorify your Father in heaven.
Matthew 5:15-16

The heart of a servant is essential to the Christian walk. It's the only true way to follow Christ's example. Jesus did not come to be served, but to serve - and if we are following Him, we will walk the same way.

We also cannot truly live out the Greatest Commandments without serving. Love is more than words; *love looks like something*. Scripture teaches us that we cannot genuinely love God, whom we have not seen, without loving our brothers and sisters we do see. One of the clearest ways love is expressed is through service.

As the Body of Christ, we have been given to one another as gifts. Many of the needs in your life are meant to be met through other believers. In the same way, you are meant to be part of the answer to someone else's needs. Often, we may struggle to move forward when dealing with our own challenges, but we find strength and clarity when we help others. By God's design, serving brings joy, because through it we reveal His heart to bless His people. When we serve, we become His hands and feet on the earth.

Just like the human body, each believer has a different function. Sometimes we wonder why someone seems strong in one area but struggles in another. This is because we are not all meant to function the same way. If my eyes stop working and I try to read with my hands, something is wrong. While it may be possible, it is inefficient and not how the body was designed to function. Each part works best when it stays in its proper role. In the same way, the Body of Christ functions best when each person serves according to how God designed them.

Many people feel overwhelmed because they want to help everyone, everywhere. That can feel impossible - like trying to find a single lost penny somewhere in the entire world. But when you know your people and your place, service becomes much clearer and more manageable. God doesn't call us to serve everyone the same way or to be everything to everyone, but He does call us to faithfully serve those He has placed around us.

Serving is also a form of worship. Scripture teaches that everything we do should be done as unto the Lord. This means that even simple, unseen acts - such as setting up chairs, washing dishes, or cleaning bathrooms - can be acts of worship when done with the right heart. When we serve others, we are serving God.

There are different levels or capacities in which believers serve:

- **Fruit** is the evidence of the Holy Spirit at work in every believer's life. All believers are expected to bear fruit as they walk in faith and obedience.

- **Gifting** refers to areas where someone naturally operates with strength or effectiveness. These are given by the Holy Spirit as He chooses.

- **Calling** goes a step further. A calling includes fruit and gifting, but it also involves a God-given motivation and responsibility to equip and serve others in that area. For example, someone may teach well, but a person called as a teacher carries a deep desire to help others understand and grow in God's Word.

Fruit flows from our new nature in Christ. Gifting is distributed by the Holy Spirit. Calling reflects the purpose God has placed on a person's life. All three work together, and all of them are meant to be expressed through a servant's heart.

The gifts are not meant to draw attention to us like special superpowers. They are great equalizers. For one person, they may naturally observe an imbalance in someone's posture or walk. Another person may not naturally observe that but may notice the Lord saying to heal that person. Now, if they were a doctor or chiropractor, they may be able to heal that person naturally, but if that is not the case, the Lord may heal that person strictly through prayer.

The point is that it's not for entertainment or show. It's for people to be ministered to in the name of Jesus. Ministering is simply sharing the heart of Jesus and is not always from a pulpit. It can be as simple as giving someone a cup of water. Doing something *in his name* means doing it the way Jesus would, the way he taught you. So we want to be obedient to Jesus and minister to those who need it. The focus is never the person or the gifting. The focus is glorifying Jesus, and the Holy Spirit is more faithful to do that than we are.

At the foundation of every role in the Body of Christ - no matter the function - is servanthood. Without it, we miss the heart of Jesus.

What is the Fivefold?

So Christ himself gave the apostles, the prophets,
the evangelists, the pastors and teachers,
to equip his people for works of service,
so that the body of Christ may be built up
until we all reach unity in the faith
and in the knowledge of the Son of God
and become mature,
attaining to the whole measure
of the fullness of Christ.
Ephesians 4:11-13

The modern Church has been heavily focused on teaching and pastoring, placing too much of the weight of responsibility on the backs of a small few and narrowing our view. Jesus gave five main functions to the Church like five fingers on a hand, not just two with the occasional Evangelist coming through. Even if they do not go by these titles, well balanced, Spirit-led churches will usually have people who fill each of these roles as their natural passion points.

Apostolic: Asks, "What would it look like if heaven took over? Who is ready to reveal that part of Jesus to the world?" In Acts, the Apostles appointed seven men to take care of widows.

Prophetic: Asks, "What is Jesus saying about this situation? Who needs to be able to hear the voice of God?"

Teacher: Asks, "What are the universal truths of the scriptures that people need to understand in order to renew their mind and have a more Kingdom-structured life?"

Pastor: Asks, "Are my people ok both physically and spiritually?"

Evangelist: Asks, "Who needs to know about the Gospel of Jesus Christ?"

All of us naturally ask at least one of these questions. Though it does not mean that we are in that office of the Church, but that we are part of that function of the Church. Typically, the Pastoral and Teacher pieces serve more as the stabilizers of the Body, while the Apostles, Prophets, and Evangelists serve as movers. All of these are necessary for the Church to be whole and healthy.

Will This Be Hard?

See, I have refined you, though not as silver;
I have tested you in the furnace of affliction.
Isaiah 48:10

Becoming a Christian is not a one-and-done experience. You don't just accept your ticket to heaven and become a perfect human instantly while you wait. It involves a constant pursuit of being made more into the image of Christ. Everything He does and allows is for us to constantly draw closer to Him and mature to be like Him.

We were placed into this world to be representatives of God in it. Where there is chaos, we are meant to be solution bringers. A question many have is why God allows bad things to happen. When Adam and Eve were in the Garden, Satan was already there among them. So how could a good Father put His kids into the same space as His enemy and still be a good Father? There is only one real answer...

He knows His kids are more of a threat to the enemy than the enemy is to them.

Many times, we look to God to take out our giants. But God is less interested in taking out our giants for us and more interested in turning us into giant killers. God didn't kill Goliath for David. He prepared David his whole life to be able to take out Goliath. He wasn't hoping that David could take out Goliath; He *knew* David could. Likewise, we must know that God has trained us for the season we are in. When we are going through trying seasons, He is building into us the necessities for seasons to come.

The picture of gold and silver being refined in the Bible is an important one. When gold and silver is refined, as it heats up, the impurities come to the top. Many people don't like their impurities being shown. But it is actually a good thing, because then it can be scraped off. The problem is if you don't want the impurities removed. A metal worker knows when the gold or silver is pure because they can see their reflection in the metal. How much more is Jesus looking to see His reflection in us?!

This means we will continue to experience hardship as we walk with the Lord. It is a natural consequence of the growth process in a world full of choices, not a punishment. We will not experience the total absence of pain and suffering until our appointed time comes and He calls us home to heaven. However, once we receive the Holy Spirit, God is with us in all things, stabilizing us in His peace, giving comfort, offering counsel, and so much more.

Again, we must remember that the plumbline of our identity as Kingdom citizens is righteousness, peace, and joy in the Holy Spirit. That is the core of who we are, the standard we measure against. When we experience other emotions like guilt, shame, anger, or sadness, they are meant to be indicators that something has pulled us out of alignment and help us identify how to address it.

If I fall and scrape my knee, the pain I feel is my body communicating to my immune system where to target healing efforts, and it's making me consciously aware of an area I need to carefully protect while it is weak and vulnerable. You will feel some degree of pain until it is fully healed.

Emotional pain is the same. Guilt and shame point us to repentance. Anger points us to pursue justice in healthy ways. Sadness points us to heal from what is often a form of loss or unmet expectations. They are simply arrows. If you ignore or suppress what is being communicated and do not take the proper action, the feelings will get louder and more intense in order to get your attention.

When you understand what these God-given emotions were meant to do for you - make you aware of how to correct what is out of alignment so you can come back to righteousness, peace, and joy - you place the emphasis on your true identity. This removes power from the enemy to manipulate your emotions, makes it easier to process and regulate the hard moments, and gives you a clear path forward. Be quick to lay these things at the foot of the cross, letting Him clean and treat your wounds so you can heal. Be quick to let Him remove the impurities so you see His image in you.

The presence of the Lord in your life demands transformation, and like all precious things in this world (diamonds, oil, wine, butterflies, etc), your life will be pressed to produce something of higher quality. Embrace the priceless value of your old life being laid down for a better one, and be prepared for the endurance needed in the process of change so that you come out the victor on the other side. The Spirit will guide you one step at a time at a pace and in a style that is best for you.

Just keep your mind on the truth of Romans 8:31-39. You are *more* than a conqueror, and there is nothing that can separate you from the love of God. The relationship is always more important than performance. Your value is in who you are to Him, not in what you can do for Him. Because He is love and made you in His image, you will naturally begin to act more and more in line with His nature. Any bumps along the way will be small in comparison to eternity.

What Comes Next?

"I am the vine; you are the branches.
If you remain in me and I in you,
you will bear much fruit;
apart from Me you can do nothing.
John 15:5

Scripture says before the foundations of the world were laid, He knew us. He had a thought of having someone who would display His glory in a certain way into the physical realm. He wrapped that thought in skin and gave it your name. Nothing you have ever done or gone through has made Him think that less of His glory should be displayed through you. In fact, because we had all sinned and fallen short of the glory of God, He sent Jesus to die for us.

According to Ephesians 2:8-10, we are not saved *by* good works, but we are saved *unto* good works. That means there's no checklist of tasks we can do to earn the gift of salvation, but once we have it, we are meant to be compelled by the love and goodness of God to be obedient in following the Spirit in doing the good things He planned for us to do. The Lord actually expects us to bear fruit, but it is He who ultimately bears the responsibility of that. We are told to simply stay connected to Him, and in staying connected, we will bear fruit. A branch doesn't try to bear fruit. It stays connected to the vine or the trunk of a tree. The roots supply nutrients up through the vine or trunk, then through the branch, and the branch naturally bears fruit simply by staying connected.

Galatians 5:22-23 talks about the fruit of the Holy Spirit - love, joy, peace, patience, kindness, goodness, faithfulness, gentleness, and self-control. It says there are no laws against them, because fruit is not about what we shouldn't do, it's about what we should do. The Holy Spirit plants divine nature (God's character) like a seed in our heart. When we spend time with the Holy Spirit, we grow and they are naturally produced in us. The fruit is proof of walking with the Lord, a life changed, a new nature. Our character starts to look like God's character.

This is the call to discipleship, to be students and sit at the feet of our teacher. There were many who followed Jesus, but only some of them became disciples. It says Jesus only spoke to the masses in parables, but for His disciples, He would take them behind closed doors and teach them in more detail.

This book has introduced the basics of Christianity. If you have questions about it, we encourage you to reach out to us, another pastor, or a friend who has walked with Jesus for a while. Don't just leave them unanswered. The foundations are important and not meant to be rushed.

Once you feel secure in the basics, if you have found this beneficial and would like to go further, we invite you to go through "In His Image." It is our Core Discipleship materials that go more in depth for those who are hungry to learn and grow. Until then...

**The Lord bless you and keep you;
the Lord make His face shine on you
and be gracious to you;
the Lord turn His face toward you
and give you peace.**

Justin & Elly Heckel

Justin & Elly are ministry leaders, worshippers, and disciple-makers with a passion to see individuals and families transformed by the presence of God. For over 15 years, they have led worship and built teams in churches, ministries, and outreach efforts throughout the Midwest. They currently serve as Pastors of His Presence Church in Sioux Falls, South Dakota, and are actively involved in equipping others through teaching, discipleship, and community outreach.

Justin is the author of *In His Image: A Guide to Making Disciples* and brings a strong focus on spiritual formation and practical discipleship. Elly, a digital marketing and brand specialist, carries a gift for communicating biblical truth with clarity and relevance. Together, their heart is to help people build lives centered on Christ and to see the next generation rooted in faith. They are raising three sons and love serving in ministry as a family.

Ann Lenaers

Ann is an ordained Christian minister, Master Certified Life Coach, leader at *His Presence Church*, mother to Ava, and founder of *Peace Is The Road*, a ministry devoted to unity in the Body of Christ. With a passion for communication and emotional intelligence, Ann's work centers around getting to the heart of partaking in divine nature.

Through creative outlets like writing, public speaking, coaching, and music, Ann fosters an authentic, Spirit-led atmosphere for reflection and growth while motivating loving action. She believes true peace and joy are not found in circumstances, but in a relationship with God that reshapes identity, purpose, and daily living to align with righteousness, peace, and joy in the Holy Spirit. Her approach blends biblical truth with practical insight, equipping others to walk in freedom, wholeness, and Kingdom citizenship.

OUR MISSION:
To host environments of God encounters, train and equip individuals in partnering with the Holy Spirit, and unite communities to expand the Kingdom of God.

DEMONSTRATE – EQUIP – CONNECT

Learn more about how to partner with us at hispresence.net

9 7989 04 171148